Illuminations

Illuminations
A Poem

Mark Wilson

LEAKY BOOT PRESS

Illuminations: A Poem
by Mark Wilson

First published in 2016 by
Leaky Boot Press
http://www.leakyboot.com

Copyright © 2016 Mark Wilson
All rights reserved

No part of this book may be reproduced or transmitted in any form or by any means, electronic, mechanical, photocopying, recording, or otherwise, without prior written permission of the author.

ISBN: 978-1-909849-38-9

Contents

A Draft of 30 Illuminations	7
City Illuminations	39
Threshold to Threshold	71
Luminescence	99
Acknowledgements	125
About the Author	127

A Draft of 30 Illuminations

"In the gloom, the gold gathers the light against it."

– Ezra Pound

1.

To project word-cylinders of
ultra-violet from semantic precincts
of an infra-red citadel surely
> requires qualification?

Vocal throat-clearing is hardly
glossolalia, is it now? Although
seraphs may once have serenaded the
surrogate daughters of Eve upon
> this scorched threshold we
> now linger upon.

In liminal-speak this is a larynx-
impossibility. To stress meta-
physically some virginal fleshing-out
despite those virtual fleshpots,
> these over-cautious firewalls
thwarting our intended ingress into
> the Bridal Chamber.

Labial-contrivances, lethal urges
to economically announce the over-
charged, oft-molested Logos-child;
neither to stint Justice and her
> resolute retinue who, in
discreet attendance, have not uttered
> vainly a word.

2.

To be angelically overridden, thrust
into the spoilers' trench invites an
      accolade of flattering labials.

Bomberg entrenched in his Cubist
blood-mud, his organic superflux;
Lewis painting the worm-like sentry
as he emerges: a mannequin of
          spent mucilage.

We labour to emit energy and
haemoglobin; for man remains the
ruptured span of his own containment,
but certainly noble still in his own
      scurrilous slide along the hot
          rails of Hinnom.

Gertler's *Merry-Go-Round* more than
just allegorical assemblage; fairground-
screams being the routine prayers
      of holy thaumaturges.

My eager barista passes over the
balm of Gilead and all is well again
      in this kingdom of
          Vox Humanos.

3.

To torch temples and synagogues,
act the otiose religiose who is
always servile in his murderous
mastery of Fundamentalism, is
        surely a sagacious folly?

Your charred tabernacle is left
sputtering in a spliced orchard
              once Edenic.

Even the treacly apples are left
cindered in the overgrown mouth
of adolescence; for that burning
      bush never contained
           a Seraph after all.

And only spent Nostalgia, in mock
dumb-show, stalks your every
            erotic climax.

4.

Bunyan's fen-horizon spreads as far as
    allegory can theologically go.

So we pace Dantescan on this fiery
plain, keep asking rhetorical
questions to a shady troupe who, in
extreme freeze-frame, still try our
    short-fuse patience.

In memory of whom? Streamlined
requiems were reactivated then
    self-consciously 'released'.

Dunamis of wit-inscribed epigraphs
still storming Limbo's Bastille in
the small, erratic hours: a coup-de-
grace of phonemes rattling from
out the auto-suggestive mouths
    of speechless troubadours;

their sackbutts and viols still hang
in exilic lindens: strangely limp,
    utterly Goya-victim'd.

5.

Water is stealthily silent, carrier
of its own implicit light and purpose.
An invisible infiltrator filtrating the
concrete infra-structures like a plain-
clothes sniper or transparent agent
                              of reconnoitre.

No hardened surface or durable
material is impenetrable to its subtler
wiles. The rot it leaves speaks for its
own desecrated congregation; a foetid
host dissipating in the
                      evanescent light-capsules.

After the seep's deluge the plebeians
try to salvage keep-safes and
dignity. Needless to say, Vesuvius has
less venom than this
                      merciless saturation.

6.

Who broke faith? What
covenantal shattering occurred in
these secular precincts? Nonsense; we
are constantly perambulating beneath
temple apses, secluding ourselves
                              in hid divinity.

Communion is transpiring
syntactically even now. Do you
                              receive me?

And you might go looking for
Manicheans in my every clause and
declension, but you won't find any.
Nonetheless, Creation's Source
contracts and expands like the four
sacred chambers of
                              a pulsating heart.

7.

The man with the writing-case is
trying my patience; severely. He
appears at all apertures like a pent-up
angel in a pop-up book of
                      Blake's *Jerusalem*.

How much time do I have,
perennially speaking? When the
average duration of focus is the length
of an advertisement there is
                                    no chance.

True; I am playing for elusive time
despite the depressing evidence that
this is an Endgame. And it appears to
            be your move, evil doppelgänger.

8.

We are the span of our own
longevities; organic calculi,
but our harmonies still fall shy
      of the heavenly Fibonacci.

Seemingly, we have made high
religion out of our technologia;
every man's hand faithful on the
          breviary of his cellular.

Poets, prophets, promulgators of
psalms are all but superfluous
commodities, bona-fide luxuries
only for those who have the necessary
attention-spans. I is another
                after all.

And Contemplation is a heretic-
outlaw bitched to crawl her tortuous
span through the rigged apparatus of
their acute de-sensitivity and miscarriage;
but, still, it's only she who is left
           tele-visually alive.

9.

Armageddon has raged
into injury-time. We're
incontinent. Won't you
brass-blow us a breather?

10.

Render unto Caesar
only if you're *not* the
bar-coded behemoth
mounting the svelte
leviathan of the
      Caribbean.

11.

Show-time; edgy trapeze-poet
edging along a taut wire of
linguistic woe, semantic welfare;
it's as if his shortened breath-
gulps depended indeed upon
this ridiculous over-stretch of
      sheet-music shrillness.

12.

Anabasis is the formation *a la mode*.
It conceals its anarchic undertones
like a lithe serpent curtailed within
                      the smoother stone.

Lady Macbeth must be my dancing
partner for this particular sarabande;
whilst I propose that Eloise will be
next to Jericho-jig me around the
                              turreted compound.

Yes, these arch-arabesques are
merely strident teasers, but they will
not ultimately despoil the internal
                      mechanics of the thing.

Take my embossed word for it; there
is war even in the inner-plazas of
Heaven:
                only Hell is empty.

13.

So is it to be the gyres, the vortex
or the insurmountable echelons
of the empyrean to provide
    our supreme
                mental fulcrum?

If your body is the microcosm of
this whole universe, how is it you're
still panicking at the end of your
              mortal tenure?

*Mysteries to ourselves and, most
of all, to each other;* so we ideogram
our ideals into the five corners of
this pentagonal *perpetuum mobile*
and expect divine absolution as if
              by instant fiat.

Surely, Heaven's hippodrome must
be top-full of celestial laughter by
now; still surf-riding this gag-line
as potent as Halley's
            inexhaustible comet.

14.

Hewn four-square, the smooth aureates;
sculpted effortless the concave
paradigms of seraphic abdomens.
Perspectival: the serene escaliers
diminishing into a multi-dimensioned
middle-distance intractable by
                              the finite eye.

Regal niches of the fantastical rationales;
those highly-disputed thrones of
                  contingency, harsh necessity.

But: of such 'sights' we are
punctiliously rationed as we cower
within the Anderson Shelter of our
various incredulities; for only sirens
here illumine the dusty grains of
                              our petrifaction.

15.

Hoggers of harvest,
perversely insatiate bellies
hungering for a thousand
grain mountains. The

chasm has them. Materially
desensitised to the all-
fulfilling Immaterials;
Midas is their only ally.

16.

To be *lumina*; emanate glowing
particles despite our evidence of
      excrement and cloying dust.

So we wriggle heavenwards sustained
by our musty-blind fables of hell.
Athwart in this mesh of space-time,
rigged pilots of auto-choice licensed
only for solipsistic ethics and
                      self-branding.

So we slide through vitae on both
nerve and incontinence: the faster
the better. For speed only is our
oily unction, our utterly
                spent holiness.

17.

In the runnels of retinal displace-
ment this mole treadles his own
intractable tunnel; flawlessly tactile
this cylinder of inner-vision sustains
him despite the milky opacity and
        the ragged haemoglobin ribbons.

And Bartimaeus' blind faith barely
keeps him alive in this autocracy of
the dead whilst Oedipus chooses the
blind guilt of
        displacement-theory.

This scintillating iris always was the
most sensitively precious organ in
our oblique bodies; hummingbird-
wing-delicate as it flutters its green
vibrato of daring in the Cyclopic
        red-eye of the hurricane.

18.

Echo-chamber of sound and touch
imprints a cartography of sheer
acoustics; my braille bible still
bridles beneath your digits'
intuitive fumbling, but you've
comprehended far more subtly
than even some of those
                far-sighted ones.

Solidity of this ponderous
language requires intellect's
kinaesthesia. And I am still quite
lost without the dancing recognition
of your surprised caress, my
                blind amoureuse.

19.

This pulsing corona surrounds
you as well; an intuitive natural
reaction perhaps? Light being its
own residual energy-source at
altitude, a stalwart of
                      potent fragility.

As even now the illuminati fail
to meretriciously build their
metropolis atop the
                      temple-mount.

Rescind, my darkly luminous one;
you have overshot your globes
          of strident, spasmodic flame.

This heightened corona enrobes
you head to toe; for you too are
ascending your purgatory-replica
in this most appropriate, snow-
                    clad of hemispheres.

20.

There is a tranche of Ulysses
in all of us; perpetual exiles in an
eternal recurrence from and to
              the penumbra'd Source.

Democratising the dead ever since
you devoured that primal Canto, in
your adolescent vortex of pent-up
energeia; what *nekuia* of displacement
              and release was there then?

The roots still communicate one
to another; that fleshy pomegranate
telegraphically poised in Persephone's
jaundiced hand is still your fruit of
              sheer-rounded dissonance.

For I am done with fraught elegies'
elongation; this necropolis requires
refracted antiphons to dead poets
as direct as live men on the mart
discussing the price of
              wine and bread.

21.

They prognosticated your
retina could be displaced:
unswerving doctors, ophthalmic
paediatricians, savants of the eye; as
you juddered seamlessly between
wry humour and an
                      aggravated despair.

The clinic diffused your bonhomie,
left you clinically sterile, hyper-
frozen; petrified and morose your
persona shrank itself into a shy-
        sullen, malevolent-edgy creature.

Meanwhile, in this ministry of *Visual
Impairment* I scribe, annotate on the
verisimilitude of your coloboma
hours. On alternate days I receive
some benighted e-mail, some mis-
handled, misled attempt at
                      'counselling' you.

Botched Nature slinks away in
warped, sheer-face denial. Shadows
teem, *tenebrae* babbles. And the slit-
            like corona narrows.

Only hushed, metaphysical light can
now pierce through your slim interstices;
as the far-seeing Source keeps inkily
                      his own counsels.

22.

"Not to depict the visible; but to
make visible" (Klee). Take that
for a visionary-maker's
                            life-doctrine.

And all this will mean you are
hounded out of the Academy, the
Planetarium, many-roomed Ecclesia
and the gilded temples of
                            Capital.

Still, you will pulsate with the
intrinsically valuable tucked so
safely within; so invisible
                            without.

23.

The nimbus of your own corona:
faceted and comfortably 'in flame'.

For your ingrowth of radiance can
sometimes become a dull, dialectical
                matter.

'Make it new' unbuffed, unattended
to, becomes mere stuff of antiquarianism
                and paralysis;

something your *dunamis* will need to
daily administer to;

                      or relinquish.

24.

Were you lumen? Segmented,
bulbous, throbbing *lumina*;
penuriously valuable still
despite this tenebrous rupture
                        of the Word?

My word; linguistics became
almost paradoxical there. Semantics
a slippery shape-shifter lurking
characteristically in caverns of
chiaroscuro. Platonic caverns?
Hermetically-hidden recesses?
                Possibly maybe.

My oblique words remain
       hologrammatic
                            to a fault.

25.

To build light
houses of light
edifices mansions
of a wrought
stellar stuff which
only some of you
inky non-linear
pre-lapsarians of
the pulsing Source
will possibly recall
with any degree
of oscillating
confidence

26.

Hereward wreaking his fenland
havoc; subterfuges amongst mist-
haloed islands afloat upon the
teeming marshes; Oswald at Ramsey
subjugating the bestial demons,
by God! Medeshamstede splayed
      at the cackling mart.

And now that steady stream of
gowned scholars issues along the
pleasure-saturated Cam: our
'plumed elect' of Middle England
creaming the choicest rooms within
gilded offices of Academia-cum-
      Ecclesia-cum-Politeia.

Privatised hegemonies all oblivious
of Ezekiel's fire-inlaid wheels, Blake's
Golgonooza, Dante's unsolicited
      Rose-of-the-Empyrean.

27.

To choose blindness rather than
have your inner-fire doused, with
everyone still floundering
        bureaucratically around you.

Perspectival: the gain a more
renewed perspective. That view
from Escher's walled tower no less
an optical illusion than many pop-up
Jerusalems I could
                care to mention.

Chalcedony, agate, emerald; from
here the light positively scintillates
off things. Multi-various breastplate
of Aaron; the providential contingencies
            of Urim and Thummim.

Sophia is, for the materially driven,
an unappealing deity; for poets she
           remains the perfect woman.

Take that for ultimate figuration then
and sleep majestically for a thousand-
and-one-nights of healing balm
        sufficient in your alone-ness.

28.

In the darkly-sunken vaults the
gold gather-shines far more brightly;
pestilential hoards of kings, managers,
politicians and princes: a redolent
stockpile of surfeit and immured
                              intoxication.

A theft so gargantuan that it is
surprisingly opaque to most lazy eyes
of *res publica*; the alert ones having
been gouged out long before by
                              malevolent Cornwalls.

Fraud reassumes fraudulent mastery
with the legerdemain of the stock
actor switching persona-masks.
Magicians are mistaken for Magi in
this magnificent Canary Wharf
                              masquerade.

And the attentive luminaries are
condescended to, censored, blacklisted;
or, if all else fails, cajoled themselves
                              into the swindle.

And for the rest: an astigmatic
groping around in faecal-murky
                                            alleys.

29.

Ghiberti's gold-relief doors
slam shut before they even
have time to open; the

Mercy Seat levitates in
a vast storm-cloud of
unknowing; our temple

remains, for the sentence
of time, just another
sealed, upturned sarcophagus

on the spoilers' mound.

30.

Stone is foliage intimately
entwined; who knows
consummate craftsmen who

resurrected Chartres as a
Gothic tree out of
                        a bed of ash?

Faith finally animates us:
buttress-winged; artistry's seraph
beyond the quotidian
                                  grind of things.

A penman's cult-of-personality
is his ultimate, ponderous
curse; even the *poete maudite*

stuck within his dank oubliette
know this as incontestable,
                            incandescent
                                        truth.

City Illuminations

"J'ai seul la clef de cette parade sauvage."
— Arthur Rimbaud

31.

Must have done my sub-zero time in
the Hotel Splendide, each verset-slab
a self-contained whole: that convoy
      slick with poison and gospel.

Postdiluvian; at the very rupture of
language, at the very rapture of
      handed-round existence.

These mouthings: imprecations of
praise-songs spilling out of the
tilted drums with a venomous
precision; but you know all this, it's
braille-inscribed in your morning
angelus; your fingers conjugal with the
projected stuff; whilst your kinaesthetic
breviary is an *objet d'art* all-resonant,
signifying so much more than
      mere semantics.

Let me install it in the steady
      vertigo of the Alps.

32.

Metropolis-lights; Bethel's urban
gridlock. Your steaming counters
and redolent eateries project their
own nocturnal neon, amorous scents.

Scarlet predominates where the
faceted dragon visits the boudoir
              of the Madonna of Dawn.

Oriental lanterns festoon the
clandestine nest where you arouse
the atoms of the aesthete. Yellow
books open and close with the
        languor of dis-entwining avatars.

A singular rose-petal dissolves on
your intrepid tongue, yet speech is
seldom in this pagoda of the
             immaculate senses.

Your glowing body itself a Buddha
of serene climax; this levitating
        lotus: an unwithering solidus.

33.

You too traversed the highways
of epiphany, rode tramways of
                         translucency.

What do you really know in your
hydrogen unknowing? What
astrological implosions create the
                         judders of history?

Ur's obnoxious traffickers spoke
condescendingly at you; the
Tigris seethed in its toxic pollution;
nocturnal pleasure-boats groaned
beneath intoxicated scholars high
                         on pot and Zen.

Transfixed sharks levitated in tanks
of formaldehyde; a fin-de-siecle
maelstrom overtook legions in
                         their beds.

Beatrice's *décolleté* appeared
fleetingly in a seminar-cameo
foreshadowing Eleanor glimpsed at
Aquitaine; later still: her well-defined
figure pirouetting at the wedding
of Cana: a crystalline choreograph
possessing the clarity of a
                         spirit-glass.

You too euphoric with the fresh
impressionability of
                         vorticised youth then?

>   These sparks fly upward; nitrogen
> and camphor still burn rapid in their
>   gyrating vortex
>   of abdomens.

34.

The city smoulders its contumacy
of phosphor; furnaces of sheer
industrial plenitude grind out their
relentless purgatories of
                        iron and steel.

A small, rotund, turbaned figure
carrying a bindle of chattels
scurries up the charred slope followed
by two comely daughters; incest
lingers upon the sodomitical air and
dissipates like a cheap
                        perfume-spice.

The smoke thick, redolent and warm-
tangled as Astarte's pubic-grove is
horrendous and lethal. Ironworks,
wharfs and shipyards metallic with a
white heat start to either melt
                        or hallucinate.

A series of deafening blasts strikes a
dumbness; clutching tarnished teraphim
in sweat-frozen fists does not ensure
                        automatic salvation.

In the toxic distance gantries, pontoons,
Crystal Palace collapse, eventually
surrender to that torrid, insidious,
                        all-mastering atmosphere.

Blackened silhouettes also succumb
to the ash of exhaustion; when the

sun finally peeps through only a salty
after-taste and a lurid, phantasmagorical
                              dream linger.

35.

See: on mercurial horizons
        their faltering tread.

Unleashed from Vulcan's smithy,
     Urizen's mint-tyranny:

          reclaimed,
                    flame-tried.

No more a lost tribe than a
    creative cabal of

          inner-émigres returning.

Silver-etched,
      with the dross sluice-
            drained away.

The cities reabsorb,
      but do not contain them.

From the House of the Lamb
      issues their crafted,
           alternate gospel:

dogma, hegemony
        finally eschewed;

vision, honesty, love, mercy
     become their
            guiding principles;

Sophia the patroness
     of their wrought citadel.

And this light
                        is not from the sun.

36.

Exilic paeans to Jerusalem the
Golden, buried Albion, colonial
India and Pakistan, bella Roma;
And now: Latvia, Lithuania, Poland,
        the Czech and Slovakian heartlands.

As Scandinavian angle-poises illumine
each lead or inky stroke on parchment-
paper, each oiled gesture on canvas
                or glass;

still hear this inalienable antiphon:
    Everyman a virtual tourist
    Everywoman an inner-émigre.

So raise high the rusty candelabra; burn
redolent joss-sticks to Krishna or bright-
tusked Ganesh; intimately finger the hard-
glossed rosary; even kiss the
              fold-up Rublev icon;

it will establish your sacred exile
whatever the cartographer or sociologist
have preordained in their clinically-
uncircumcised offices, their cold studios
              of self-advancement.

37.

Domes and cupolas of an unimaginable
Civitas Dei transpire in the sultry
argentine atmosphere; you too will
have your gryphon's day in the pantheon
                       of kings and princes.

A flutter of phoenix disperse from the
garden of the Capitol; omens are
cold currency these days, so take this
munificent skyline as kerygmatic
charter in these dog-days, my
                                   chosen one.

And let the damned be doubly damned
despite the fact you still prefer their
unbridled, humane company so much
more than the straight faces of
                                   election.

38.

Pallas: aegis-aloft, her eyes owlish
penetrating the scrubbed lowlands
outside her steep, urbane walls; pupil-
slits trained upon the inhabitants of
the brush: those anarchic, non-conformist
freeloaders, parasites living-off
res publica, responsibility-shirkers,
arrogant beatniks with not a jot of
civic, or civilised, decency to their
           forgotten, forgettable names.

Pallas' face re-assumes Apollonian
composure within her fortified eyrie;
aegis-wings still appear gleam-plumed
           from the republican font.

Peace; for the indurated, enduring
citadel is still a calm votary at her
                      gilded throne.

39.

To beat out one's exile: the driving
ontological engine; to collate
souvenirs of sheer endurance, exhibit
alien scars: badges of a more
supreme witness; to alchemise the
Word as it comes into extreme
          incarnation: the virtù of virtues.

This mantra etched into every
oblivious atom, this ineffaceable
fingerprint of the divine artist
intuitively feeling out the work; with
every particle of inner- and outer-
space bearing opaquely that illusory
signature like the incurable wound

                    of a birthmark.

40.

Inherited birthmark of
mercury, spilt haemoglobin;

scarlet stigmatas passed
down the generational oak

like birthright-mementoes;
genetic blessings are a

contemporary curse in this
grand-dance of

>   *ex nihilo* rupturings.

41.

Even though I am no
Deucalion or Noah even

I can see the scarred delta as
she withdraws so tentative

from the misogyny of
the Deluge.

42.

The city masquerades as a Vorticist
danseuse but is, in reality, an
antediluvian behemoth prowling
insatiably along the Tigris'
                                  feverish loins.

This mythic flood has indeed
subsided, but you remain on-board
drifting drunkenly through
            civilisations, religions,
                               nano-technologies.

Propositioned outside the British
Museum by an Indian *gentilhomme*
which withdrew from your lips
that ultimate *noli me tangere* and
nothing short of the
                                Grand Refusal.

In the cataclysmic tunnels deep
beneath London Bridge, Kafka's
parabolic wheelchair still trundles
as the cortical sparks fly upwards
into the voluminous interstices of
                                Inner-Space.

Deep in the Senate's scriptorium-
labyrinth where you stumbled upon
the key to this cosmically-spinning
sideshow only to later discover a
                                far deeper void.

This city masquerades as a Vorticist
danseuse but is, in reality, an
antediluvian behemoth prowling
insatiably along the Tigris'
                              feverish loins.

43.

And will their cafes be as vibrant?

And will their dancing women be as
    clear-cut in beauty and poise?

And will we see Albion in their
        commuters' eyes as they pour

    from out of Charing Cross Station?

And can they *really* heal my hurt mind
    in their House of the Lamb?

44.

They've bulldozed the arena of our
brief love to build another
        subterranean station;

they've bulldozed the place of our
slow dance, O Amoreuse, for the
        blank-eyed commuters.

How easily you aligned yourself
        to my body and mouth:

an experienced Aphrodite gently

inducting her Anchises into the
        radiant Mysteries.

And that brief hour of immortality
        will not be taken from me.

45.

Nocturnals were restless as
heated night-pumas; Goldengrove's
primal antiphonals amidst the
lianas deep within that low-lit,
cavernous basement beneath
                          Regent Street.

There will come no more the
lovely ladies strapped in burlesque-
exquisite gowns, the gamely
androgynes or velveteen performing-
artistes doing their Faustian thing
in that arboreal, effervescent
                                splendour.

No more their blistering cupolas.

And no more their
                phosphorescent sound.

46.

Admit it; Gomorrah flayed you, fleeced you. Dominatrix: the slurried, seething entrails of her transportation's a bitch to navigate, generosity of her favours always extrapolating far more in return: cruel,
                      unsatisfactory *redemptrix*.

Etiolated, jejune after your excruciating "tup" between those apocalyptic prisms jutting up and down most imperiously. A botched "making" beyond contingent
                      farce or tragedy.

Beneath your bloodless fingernails an icy impedimenta of your stillborn epic writhing nakedly unseen still in the Pascalian abyss: superfluous ur-cantos, a *disjecta membra* or, at best, an embarrassing
                      posthumous-appendix.

47.

Beyond this:
           her designated orchid.

Beyond that:
           his iridiscent pearl.

Another spent Beatrice surfeited
    in the mode of some
                    Grand Refusal.

Another minor poet divinely
    abandoned to these

           grains of oblivion.

48.

Meanwhile, outside the city's
fortification grows Yggdrasil: the
five mouths of fructification or the
intelligent light as it dances in
                          photosynthesis;

a silent host building their
luminous ships, sun-forging their
scintillant caravels to transcend
the tsunami-lords of today
                          and tomorrow.

49.

Look: this metropolitan lantern with
its curvaceous sweep of fluorspar
bridges, floodlit cathedrals (which are
distilled microcosms of multi-various
Edens) ultimately are taken for
                                    granted?

Even these replicas of seraphic
throne-rooms in all their minute
vastnesses have become utterly
                          mundane and featureless?

Weren't you warned? The man who
wrote *Civitas Dei* was a priggish, guilt-
crippled neurotic ranting against an
                          imaginary brood of savages?

Hierarchy petrifies into hegemony: the
structured centre of Metaphysics can
only hold for a moment. And, inevitably,
we are subsumed in the stink of yet
                              another Deluge.

50.

Tenements, turrets and helmeted
palisades rear up as phallic reminders
    of our strange berthing;

we are the self-procurers of our own
        customised apocalypses.

And you must be out there somewhere:
a changeling-infanta discovering
    herself upon the scorched plain;

some castellated queen yawning herself
through the already-outmoded,
contemporary array of liveried jongleurs,
'reality' gleemen who pontificate
                without shame.

So we are responsible for all our hybrid-
psychological entertainments; as we
project, deny, fantasise our Edenic
replicas with a subconscious, automatic
ease that belies this ultimate
          noli me tangere.

This implicit, fundamental chemical-
bond: supreme covenant of our twisty

            commitment-vows.

51.

At certain hours, at certain points
within this urban-mesh the light is
almost perfected; something which
plebeians and aesthetes almost always
        miss or hugely under-appreciate:

some grande-maistre of lumiere achieves
a grand synthesis through aerial filters
or celestial lenses unknown which
should teach any woman or man that
        sublime craft of cinematography.

I am convinced that Tarkovsky knew
this as he sculpted poetry from filaments
of projected lumen, his non-linear
return to star-origins almost avatar-like
        in the Cold War crepuscular.

Small wonder that icons and altarpieces
radiate or pulse with this kind of solar
energy; for their creators too must have
known this harmonic welding of
        superb flame.

52.

Altar-slab to Moloch in some
crusty back-street upper-room-
      eucharist mise-en-scene;

salacious smile convinces
hapless guilt to "conveniently"
transfer herself onto
"anonymous" latrine-flushed,
              foetal scapegoat;

programmed to incontinence
still Asrael's simply unable to
secrete sap or "pass over" this
      tableau of "resolution"

53.

Emanation:
        the Source's
                pouring out

    mystere
                chain-of-being

yearn-for-return
                    god-stuff

in all the
    living beings
            of the hierarchy

empyrean-petal'd
    despite conflicted
                dark-matter

imponderability
      of our
            language-mesh;

Zyklon B
      beneath everything
    in the
      liquid compression
      of the
          plunged
              ash-pit

54.

Eight-coigned; with the octahedron
lowered perfectly. Bride-lifted, hovering
over the burnish of our splendid
                                      threshold.

The resplendent lilies self-create
pneumatic pads of landing for her:
their spiritualised physical-theatre
an organic throne. Consummation
                imminent on the bowered rooftops.

Agape-cum-eros and the rites of
hospitium. Shekhinah-divested; so the
vision falters. And the City resents
her maidenhead, her foreign lovers'
attempts at forbidden intimacy which
                can only confound and tantalise her.

Whilst the long-desired, mystical
bonding and the biochemical covenant-
of-covenants remain the mislaid stuff
                    of childhood, fiery legend.

55.

Leaving the City of the toxic
plain, that well-irrigated tidal-
basin he summoned up a basilisk
of brute determinacy, a daemon
        of self-discipline to attend him.

As the tarnished rooftops of Woolwich
dissipated into the stark urban-tunnel
reeking of petroleum, he determined
that neither euphoria or melancholia
                  had ever existed.

An indifferent season of level-
headed envisioning
                awaited him.

Threshold to Threshold

"Es war Blut, es war,
was du vergossen, Herr.

Es glanzte."

– Paul Celan

56.

Upon the burnish of one threshold
you impatiently linger; others await
      your tenacious footfall.

Watch the Angel of the Presence
hover towards you: non-apparitional,
rather nimbus-sartorial its solid-
thewed body in folds of cream
              and sapphire.

God may be silent; but, beyond
gender, Metatron sings a glossolalia
without grammar. We curtail the
god-in-us whilst elevating the naked
      red *adam* demonstratively.

For we are most intimate in our
strangeness; communing at speech-
grilles, slammed gates of impasse; our
ex nihilo confessionals impossibly
myth-embroidered,
    fable-enshrined
            and -embedded.

Redaction our credo of realisation then,
our liminal wish-fulfilment. Cunningly-
spun tribal tales that are compendious
to a contrived fault; proof-read,
suddenly archival: the (said)
              denouement.

57.

In the effulgence, Sister; where you
play with dark matter. "Jouissance",
your claustral name, certainly becomes
you as a foil; where, in the colonnades'
chiaroscuro, I seek for,
      and find, you.

Not much, my love, is
    incontrovertible then?

Look, these pressed parchments of
truth finally fly open; we inhale the
redolent fumes as if they were genuine
      messianic myrrh.

For still you're an inebriate of satin's
suggestive chic, seduced by the
mixed spices of glamour; whilst I
surrender to the poet's printed page,
the warbling lute and the sensuous
icon as if, composite, they were life's
very lexicon; all ready to envision,
    transcribe, breath-sing...

Still, upon this threshold, we fell
      together.

58.

One must wrestle the doppelgänger-
dweller; yes, one must wrestle.
Overcoming is overt in the unfurling
script; Epstein's *Jacob* our
                        exemplar and paradigm.

But you twist so; all ligamental-
prolific with the unexpected slam-to.
We breathe fresh exhaustion into
our diurnal water-jugs; seize
                        the full-nimrod.

And for the rest: a flurry of
bastinados, arpeggio-ricochets that
leaves one dweller bipedal, upright:

constellation-livid, full-frontal as
                        the two Ajaxes.

59.

Sanctums: internal; external.

Hunks of powdery bread passed
between pallid hands; ruby port
sipped down during that sparse feast
        celebrating Agape's love-child.

Sapphire baldachins with gold-
projected stitchings, snatched glimpses
of the exquisitely in-prime, Italianate
woman; her curvatures of grace are
restrained appassionatas that promise
such a gradual eastering in all the
                  scriptors' loins.

And they have brought myrrh,
incense and golden bars to adorn this
drab tableau; their black steeds, gold-
harnessed, snort impatiently into the
            morning's moist turquoise.

60.

So; fructified Yggdrasil belongs
to Nobody? The No-One's Tree
shooting out a negation of branches,
stretching its inversion of almond
        branches over our absences?

Photosynthesis occurs within the
sterile intangibilities of inner-space;
hence its pro-creativity's
        everlastingly ensured.

I am fertile only because I have
first endured
        seasons of barrenness.

61.

Patience; have sun-built up to
these apocalyptic beasts: leonine,
ramping, snuffing at numinous
                            thresholds.

Indeed, you have been patient until now
considering all the visual stimulants
        that sap your attentiveness.

For their feral wisdom is the antidote
to the bureaucracy of the infernal
machine which, with codified and
pedantic clicks, anaesthetises communion,
        desolates the supreme eucharist.

For the beasts' implicit "otherness",
within a corona of spun particles,
is strangely endearing; incisor-breath
        is both balm and spice of Eden.

62.

Oscillation is the golden-rule;
wheels amid wheels: superb; and
the spinning gyres slot into their
predecessors with an utmost, a
                    Dantescan precision.

We ride the arabesques despite our
propensity for linear-narrative; the
curvilinears are caveats of self-
discipline usually quite beyond our
                    vertical powers.

Curvy space, rotational time the
bi-luminous topos then. Keep that
in your diurnal lexicons without a
complaint-scribble; these hours are
where you will discover brilliant,
mislaid pearls; that phosphorescent
                    throb of the bulging acorn:

an alienable music of ultimate
                          homecoming.

63.

In their palatinates of ice, past
their casuistic towers:

they move
              imperceptible...

inaudible their
          ear-splitting
                    shibboleths...

unfathomable their hard
     creeds etched in
              krypton...

incontrovertible their
     marmoreal
              eschatologies...

For this was an immoveable
people who groaned in wordy
tabernacles until, void of any
humanitas, they castigated their
beloved opponents within eternal
              flame-blizzards;

their aspiration to be the very
              flail of Yahweh.

We also, for them, assume the
urns of anathema:
                  a tribe stillborn.

64.

Re-assume your god-particle in
this designated zone;

liminally speaking you are
almost whole   intoning through

speech-grilles your submarine
musicologies.   Jona-Messias

your co-partaker in these deciduous
festings   foreshadowing Calypso's

coves of etched erotica; cobalt
gesturing of an unsolicited seascape;

yet another leviathan of poetics
to be shelved in your pluperfect

dossier of epic-slant Exile.

65.

Internship of fools; calamitous.

Amber-shot: the extreme paralysis
riding, centaur-hard, up their
                              abdomens.

So they re-enact the frozen *dunamis*
of a thousand deluges.

This choreograph of stasis still
their symmetrical paradox, carving

out their own petrifaction with sub-
        zero gleet of the gorgon.

A ponderous reckoning in Cocytus
may, or may not,
                          await their plunge.

66.

Breaking black bread in the
provinces; sipping wine's
                         embittered fruit.

Beating out one's exile with
stringed instruments; inditing
onto a parchment-scroll whisked
away from the pre-abominated
                         temple.

Sonic-boom flagellates our
abandoned landscape; we inhabit
Nash and Ballard's country where
the technological horizon exudes
                         its luminous carbon.

Their paltry vision has become
even narrower: a stubborn nail
                         ingrown.

67.

Luminescence: the vision crystalline
in all its multi-faceted "otherness".

Artistic men and women prone to
rapture kneel, then conceive
                        miracle-monads.

Edenic children reign from their
thrones of sapphire attended by
transcendent beasts all pad-foot on
                    the pneumatic sward.

As levitating seraph-dancers, gold-
brocaded, choreograph themselves in
the way that sepals are, Fibonacci-
              wise, arranged in nature.

And the sibyls' poised facial-ecstasy
              is untranslatable...

Gradually the man-with-the-writing-
case tugs at my sleeve; matter
re-assumes its cloying mastery on
this lower-rung of spent
                          hierarchy.

68.

God-in-us ponders
murkily the downward
heave of matter;
despite the chain-mesh
subconsciously yearns
for prodigal re-immersion;
darkness-visibility's
shroud self-surprises
with an incipient
luminosity of sudden
Source-coming.

69.

Has the six-winged lion carved out
his chiasmus? Pinion-perfected, his
    feline aerodynamics stun.

We pause; dread agape.

Authority comes from such right-
    reasoned visions, so you opine.

Fulvid: its magisterial fur.

Watch the six-winged bull, eagle
and man circle behind him each
    in their own wise.

Still, there are no shadows feathered
    across this muted threshold.

Light not of the sun.

70.

If transmigration is our passage;
if the vibration of the thousand things
causes this particular threshold to
appear most permanent; if we are
cyclically construed for god-fulfilling
purposes; it's something far beyond
the online saws of soothsayers
                             and sibyls.

Seventy-times-seven should be your
acts of mercy; daily your splitting
of jars containing olibanum and
                      sweetest myrrh.

An altar-stone of jade flickering
within every room; this unorthodox
text just another page in the moveable,
                      the most-virtual lexicon.

Trial-by-fire; who really is to say
what part of you will bust through the
cosmic sea of *via lactea*; what other
translucent lintels will welcome you;
                        or, maybe, shun.

71.

Mica-eyed,
womanly radiance upon
my idiosyncratic
threshold.

Seems like your
tantalizing particular is
my unshakeable
universal after all.

For there is none like
you in the thoroughfares,
in the precincts of this
ineluctable temple.

None with such exquisite hands!

Their scarlet proscenium
has not flourished for us
a suitable encomium.

Our bodies' mystery
quite possibly this song's
all-pervading *mysterium*.

Whereas the history of
our communion has been
more akin to the *henosis* craved
by flesh-starved mystics.

As soul animates your
gorgeous thighs, flamelets
lick effusively at the
lintel above us.

Inluminatio coitu always a script more resonant than credo.

Whilst I patiently await, beneath these six wings, the ultimate slow-train of your consummation.

72.

All gates are holy
All thresholds are sanctified
The lintel is our covering
as we enter *atasal*

73.

Each fresh tesserae slab's a
tabula rasa; the John the Baptists
      of your incipient *vita nuova*.

First light: incontestable, so
hierarchically-charged; the mosaic
aflaring its non-signifying other.

Duccio perceived this as he
      painted the *Maesta*.

Sandro, gold-illumining his intricate
dance of angels, instinctively
enacted that
      choreography of thrones.

Time enough to marvel; for space
abounds abundantly within this
almost-forgotten
      dimension of stillness.

74.

Descending scale, Fibonacci-
wise; so we measure accordingly
each to the proportion of our
      own fig-tree and threshold.

The Fugue builds itself upon its
own oppositions; paradoxically
harmonic the golden *ad parnassum*
gleams its wrought contradictions
      all rhyme-flagrant.

Meanwhile, architectonics of
non-light's buoyancy scintillate
      like an oil-luminous moonscape.

From our murky grottoes we
palatially envision the ascending
scales; but, from such luminaries,
always keep our
          scaly distance.

75.

Must I re-write the annals
with a stylus of impure flame;
nib-scorch histories, fables
      and the like?

Your redaction has indeed got
the better particle of you, the
worst is still lurking beneath
tribal lintels: hovering, all
                wraith-incoherent.

Demand metamorphosis
Demand a journey to the dead
You are interred within an
even blacker wood; but at
least you're still intelligent enough
                to grow.

76.

Furry assemblage, return of
the sacrosanct creatures. Hot
breath on thigh, hot breath
                       on ankle.

Leonine splendour's still
                a frisson electrical.

Incisor-pulse:
                grove of Circe
                grove of the Edenic Eve;

those throbbing laburnums
big with the intelligence
                of sap.

Forsake me not.
No, not in John's darkest hour;
                leave me not.

Yet in my negation is the ignition
of a most translucent
                        Alba.

77.

Ultimate configuration; the
new assumption? Emerald of
mesmerism, monumental in
      velocity:

Beata Beatrix as Rossetti had
envisioned her "in the mind
      eternal" (blood-enthroned).

With Lord Love, the gilt sundial
and the bridges jumping over
the Thames rather than the Arno.

Ah, what polluted congregation
      of waters, Lizzie;

whilst your laudanum-stained
threshold becomes a subsumed
      bird-of-passage.

And the angel hover-lurches
away with its sprained ankle,
      its punctured wings.

And, left behind, you are quite
resplendent, positively in the
      liminal.

78.

Incarnation; the body domiciling
inside the soul. Transit: a flitting
of larks ascending despite of/
                within the radiance.

Dimensions of a further speed or
stillness await the temerity of
                our naked foot-falls.

Nature's celestial kaleidoscope
opens her oblique apertures: a
macro-cosmic citadel; the resulting
commerce is always transacted in
                    holiness.

79.

To bust out of the cosmos, to
enter over the higher thresholds:

to maintain the ultimate henosis?

How can the acolyte prosper then
within a deluge of technologia
being harried by the Earthshaker,
        grand-master of barcodes?

Conditioned to the one synthetic
realm; commodified to non-
ambitious visions, thrashing about
in the unconditional stews of
              relativity.

So: dangerous muse, queen over
my idiosyncratic Phlegethon; how
come only your herbs, ichor and sass
       have the power to stir me now?

Your spun acetates of light my
       most discreet chrysalis.

80.

Circe-Calypso: I am your
hapless detainee willing to be
your aroused captive, unwilling to
    yield a negative fecundity.

This threshold stained with olibanum
and metaphysical blood; the
nihilistic lilt of your game within my
    trashed *paradiso terrestre*.

Luminescence

"Poca favilla gran fiamma seconda."

– Dante Alighieri

81.

Miraculous possibility of
Earthly Paradiso drove on the
isolated visionaries; their foresight
of a marvellous Syon-Roma that
glimmers typographically within
        the poem's middle-distance.

Chalcedony thrones of the just
rulers are placed like phyllotaxis
within leaves: true cosmic
        proportions of *Iustitia*.

Luminous fortifications are the
very pattern of a heavenly city.
Exemplar-template of grace,
        equality and fruitfulness.

Distribution of goods in fair
accordance as a measure of work
done: a Byzantium of self-
sufficiency with the temple kept
        holy, all commodity-free.

In short: an incandescent city
that literally emanates forms of
        the Eternal.

82.

In that juridical garden beyond
Lethe where you receive hot
            feminine fulmination.

Behind the placid gryphon and
between the cardinal virtues
                  dancing as a triad.

Dance away, Matilda;
      leave me here, Petra-Pomona.

Are we able to choose what we
remember, what we misremember?

Elms of paradise; Sandro and
      Sebastian in deep colloquy;

arboreal architectonics; ultimate
reconciliation in a glistening
                  arbour.

And the light continues to pour
            from no star or sun.

83.

In this self-watered garden
where we levitate:

her in contrapposto, with the
dawn-light sculpting out the
      sacred grove:

           a solid dimension.

We are marginally beyond holy
texts, dogmatic charisma and
           the like.

Lapis atmosphere our true
             clothing.

Attuned to the mystical, perhaps
the quasi-henosis; jointly
      bathed in the Source's light.

Scintillant: the cupped
      hemispheres of white.

Escalation soft upon the thermals;
projected agate-gleam from
           the brilliant iris;

      pirouetting, together rising.

Soon everything is in third-angle
orthographic, multi-dimensional;

as if partially perceiving the
Cosmos through intelligent
           Designer's eyes;

   pneumatic bodies ariel-lifted
      supra matter by Soul;

this:
   the mystic's inaugural
        freighting.

84.

Plotinus opining that the model
is always cyclical; heavenly
bodies circumvolving back to
                their Source.

The rest: an interpenetration
(through various degrees) of
luminosity-cum-intelligence
depending on their escalier's
                        placement.

Even you have become ecstatic
on odd occasions; as if abruptly
god-domiciled (at 5 am in the
               morning for instance).

Iamblichus saw an array of
heavenly creatures between, all
partaking in their places within
              that supreme gradation.

Ezekiel and Dante not alone then
in seeing these sublimer beings.

For you were within a whisker
of paradise that honeyed afternoon
all replete with Botticellian
imagery, the Red Priest's aural
                           contribution.

And that sacred conversation
in the dawn-hours always worth
               keeping awake for...

And its tawny muzzle-breath on
    your nape so restorative...

And your tongue a miracle of
divine syncopation; always a
vibrant reed of restraint in Love's
    vast polyphony.

85.

Aero-paradigmatics then;
Contemplation's flight-path:
becoming one with the object
        focused upon.

We live (possibly) for such
                effulgences?

The rest: a fumbling in inky
workshops or egotistical denials
        in suspicion-shaded garrets.

And then suddenly the chink
finally widens; maybe for an
        epic milli-second;

enough to glimpse the phos-
phorescent rungs: foreshortened,
ascending, eventually dissipating
           beyond our finite vision.

86.

And to cultivate mystic lilies, to
claim and/or proclaim a higher
justice surely our overriding
                       topos then?

You who have lived within a
CAD-CAM stage-set reveal now
                       your true persona;

subtly daubed with unguents of
Chanel: gleaming white, virtually
flawless; my paradisical honey
                       unconsummated.

Maybe I have set you up to a
slight degree although *virtu* is
                       only marginally conflicted here.

Still, our twinning's beyond
divine check or reprimand; bruised
magnets energy-sublimating
                       those cosmic force-fields.

Rosa Mystica,
                       Petra-Pomona;

meet me some clear day sepal'd
                       ecstatically in our Empyrean.

87.

Paradise is, semantically
speaking, difficult. Elysium a
trickier landscape for the tone-
> painter to ease out.

Sunlight can be replicated in
every galaxy, but the Source-light
that is ineffable, let alone
> unfathomable.

Celestial bodies must filter that
original glow with varying degrees
through the many
> stratospheres;

even you are a receptacle, or
crucible, containing filament-
shards of light; part of life's
mysterium is the demonstration of
how to refract that
> luminosity on.

88.

It is to the supreme dance I'd
bring you, to the weave of their
celestial choreograph as they
sarabande to appropriate
Vivaldian rhythms:
         basso profondo.

Each knowing the station of
their own idiosyncratic flux
within the ampler overall harmony.
Almost, as if with lasers, they
cleanly splice Botticellian
         firmaments;

hieroglyphic lanterns that can
only scan God's Grammar with
extreme flexibility and measured
         restraint.

Almond-white: their exquisite
arms and legs in
         adroit arabesque.

Their economic concentration-
cum-luminosity can only dumbfound
the already glutted-blind, materially-
         fallen crew.

89.

That acorn of light positively
swelled when the book was opened;
the script's luminosity beyond
      proscription or inerrancy.

The flamelets of logopoeia inter-
lacing in their intricate chaconne:
      unmoving, never still.

Song-maps of an Earthly Paradiso,
microcosms of an eternal Neo-
platonic Garden; Ezekiel and Dante
transposed by
      Plotinus and Pound, maybe.

Ancient Vorticism: the six exalted
wings our sacral covering as we
encounter the effulgence of
      effulgences.

Syon-Roma with a cupola or two
from Byzantium, maybe a brocaded
willow-garden from Beijing; some-
thing, at any rate, both
      Oriental and Occidental.

Something all humankind can
sincerely plant belief in...

Something that satiates the freighted
      god-in-all-of-us...

Something that makes, like the
ripening sepals,
      pregnant sense.

90.

Someone needs to call up to
the poet-pilgrim, whether he's
building his Nehemiah-walls, his
Tempio Malestiano or his
Empyrean pleasuredome, surely
he won't remain up there:
Beatrice-swooning, all light-
                          inebriated?

He's not the first visionary artist
and, by a long piece of chalk, he
                won't be our last.

The replica of heavenly cities
translated onto Earth is an edgy,
abstruse business which puts
the arcane back into
                        the *arcanum*.

The Gaza Strip: a bombsite of
internecine carnage, civilian limbs,
        religio-fundamental hatred.

Primed financiers in goggles
jockey into position for the finest
3D-aerial views; cross-sectional:
these minarets and turrets of
                premeditative slaughter.

Whilst mercenaries and torturers
arrive *en masse* as if by proxy. Not
far behind: knowing publicists,

leering journalists and photographers
scramble within a hellish blaze of
lumen artificiel:

    Hell's uncontained paradise.

91.

And so paradise is, undoubtedly,
splintered, shining only in
visionary fragments: piecemeal, a
tantalising prospect rather than
                     an enjoyed realisation.

Luminous traces, hardly the norm,
that occasionally surprise, spur
                     on the curious questers:

a good wine, a shapely thigh, an
        act of unbridled mercy.

Sometimes poetry itself has
embodied the litany-scrolls of
                             rapture.

92.

Wherever one perceives oneself
upon this escalator of Amor will
be according to individual
                          mind-station.

Demographic of paradise: a state
of mind rather than a geographic
                          location.

And still the light pours, infiltrates
bodies (celestial or otherwise). No
        use in denying it any more.

Even darkness knows itself to be
visible to the enlightenment of
                          some oculists.

For, under certain planetary spheres,
the incandescence bulges beyond
measure. We see it for what it is;
                or we do not see.

Under certain influences the cords
of luminescence emit counterpoint;
whilst some do not, some hear it for
what it is and are gladsome
partakers in an
                          Edenic plainsong.

93.

The projected light is the healing
word spoken at the most propitious
                            moment.

The light projects in renewed
time, within re-sculptured space.

Exteriors within shimmering
exteriors; glowing installations that
defy the eye's temporal-spatial
                            expectations.

The city which is built wholly from
Source-light appears from here to
be hewn from purest glass or
                            chalcedony.

Is this too much? Or not enough?

Sometimes even well-chosen
words prove a kind of trespass or
                            violation.

94.

Your injured mind healed in
the temple of jade; your reason
re-immersed into the heavenly
                            Nous.

Lethe rinsed away all Freudian
impedimenta. And you rose,
acolyte-fresh, a child-monarch
of sorts buoyed on *apocatastasis*
                        rather than apocalypse.

The universal forms as your
recurring template then; a cyclical
model as opposed to the
                        fundamentalist linear.

And the cosmos remains forever
a vortex of spinning emanations
perpetually recharged at the
                                Source.

95.

Each individual being within
its hood of nimbus-flame;
heavenly auditors, each with a
    regal bearing peculiar to itself.

And indeed the pilgrim possesses
the tongues to converse mellifluously
    with each-and-every one of them.

These ariel-parchments of
glossolalia: contained breath,
liberated mind-chansons that create
vast cantatas of interactive
                          praise.

Yet still having true discernment
to know the right time to feel the
    sanctity of silence.

96.

Confess it; you're dizzy,
>
> nauseous even.

The ascent has been tortuously
oblique, virtually an hermetic
telescope which utterly convolutes
the transcendent cosmos into a
>
> condensed micro-cosmos.

Your pupils dilate, turn inward.

I, too, have had occasional doubts
over the flashy projection of such
a lurid *Commedia*-kaleidoscope as it
slots itself upon unmapped
>
> negative-space.

Maybe the stars themselves implore
>
> a kind of just protestation?

Maybe I have invented new
mysteriums, created fluorescent
moon-alps for astronaut-cranks to
>
> mountaineer up?

Maybe the patient reader needs to be
>
> more, or less, than 'gentle'?

Maybe the patient reader is, under
certain circumstances, allowed to
engineer the
>
> 'death of the author'?

97.

Light, light of my eyes;
permeate my being, circulate
through the close cavities, the
                narrow canals.

Teach translucence; instruct me
in those hallowed arts of refraction
                and photosynthesis.

Break through the Ego and the Id;
as I watch the opaque-filter
absorb, before it practises virtuous
                dissemination.

A sheath of light, indeed you are
an unfailing muse of fluidity and
                dynamism.

You silently envelop my being
with effervescent clothing. Now,
dignified, I stand upright within
                your providential harbouring.

The rest of our union is, quite
succinctly: a post-textual
                levitation.

98.

Perpetual light builds from out of
itself; there is a sacred architecture
at work here:

organic, super-conscious,
                          all Fibonacci-efficient.

For, in this city-republic, we
have no need of mayors or
                          town-planners.

All authority, all liberty proceeds
from the Source far quicker than
even the vortex of
                          illumination.

99.

And your illumination shall
        proceed your incarnation:

As scintillating syntax is
inscribed with the raised
              stylus-of-flame...

As the semi-quavers sing their
own ideogrammic presences
              into being...

As the released tongue is
disabused of inspiration's
molten coal and infused instead
              with paradisical honey...

As the healed chambers of the
heart pulse with a cosmic
notation, their transcendent
              rule-of-four...

As tireless Amor choreographs
the stars and the Primum Mobile
in their ineffable, their
              cyclical sarabande...

As the entire chain-of-being
receives the Source-light with
varying degrees of intelligence
              and/ or contemplation...

And your illumination shall
always proceed your
              resurrection.

100.

In some senses an arduous
pilgrimage through ice, shit and
fire to glimpse the floodlit
Espaliers resonating with
                Agape and purpose.

There's no real point, at this stage,
of a backward glance though; only
a projected gleam forward can be
                desirable.

In some senses this might merely
be a preliminary reconnaissance;
the alternate realities must be,
                are measureless.

Still, it's been enlightening, even
corrective;
                just to suggest.

Soul *into* Nous *into* Source;
another treatise temporarily beyond
        this particular typeset-ink.

An interleaved intaglio or two
              wouldn't go amiss?

Infra-red, ultra-violet: something
              more sustainable perhaps?

As I return, super-ordinarily, to
temporal light:
                this sun.

Acknowledgements

Thanks to: James Goddard, Seb Doubinsky, Paul Stubbs, Blandine Longre, Andrew O'Donnell, Will Stone, Michael Lee Rattigan, Jos Roy, Sarah Roberts, Patrick Anderson, Suzanne Norman, Jenny Warner, Martin Cibik, Andrew & Hannah Pattison and my parents.

About the Author

Mark Wilson has previously published three poetry collections: *Quartet For the End of Time* (Editions du Zaporogue, 2011), *Passio* (Editions du Zaporogue, 2013) and *The Angel of History* (Leaky Boot Press, 2013). His poems and articles have appeared in *The Black Herald, The Shop, 3:AM Magazine, The Fiend, Epignosis Quarterly, International Times* and *Le Zaporogue*.

www.ingramcontent.com/pod-product-compliance
Lightning Source LLC
LaVergne TN
LVHW041546070426
835507LV00011B/947